I0067179

Mastering
the
Sales Process

by Jay Butler

AssetProtectionServices.com

ISBN 978-0-9914644-6-3

MASTERING THE SALES PROCESS

THRIVING ON 100% STRAIGHT COMMISSION

Table of **Contents**

Disclaimer

Preface

My name is Jay Butler and I have successfully operated in a 100% straight commission sales environment since 1993. This book is intended to provide you with the most useful sales skills, strategies and techniques I have employed in both the inside and outside sales arena. Knowing less than 10% of all people read past the first chapter of any book, I hope you find the inspiration to "learn from those who do" and study the content throughout this publication. There is 'no fluff' contained within these materials and I believe the concentrated information will prove invaluable in both your personal life and sales career.

Acknowledgments

While attending Boston University the adage "those who can't do - teach" was abundantly clear and I realized that traditional forms of education were not going to provide me with the keys to success I sought. Additionally, paying for my mounting student loans was quickly becoming a reality. I knew it wouldn't be easy to go out into the workplace and 'get that first job' and so my quest began to improve myself and my understanding of people to better increase my chances of being hired upon graduation.

My sales career began selling tickets for a company called "Achiever's Network International" which sold seasonal tickets to live presentations for a variety of keynote speakers such as Dennis Waitley, Mike Ditka, Pat Riley, Zig Ziglar, Les Brown, Tom Hopkins and Jim Rohn. My intention at the time was to learn as much as I could. I used the proceeds from my sales to purchase all the presenter's materials at a discounted rate from the company. Being a college student and new to the world of sales, I was delighted to have such an opportunity as I simply couldn't afford the thousands of dollars required to purchase their materials at retail.

The company wound-up being mismanaged and filed bankruptcy owing me what, at the time, was a considerable amount of money. But the compensation of discounted materials from the presenters helped off-set my losses and, if there were any out-standing debts owed to me, I have long since been repaid with the knowledge and experience gained. I am still grateful to this day for that door having been opened as it gave me access to a world of possibility.

I later travelled around the country to a number of cities as a volunteer for Anthony Robbins. Some college students chose to follow the Grateful Dead, I chose to tour with Tony. Although I cannot say I knew Mr. Robbins personally, at the time he did at least know my name and would say hello to me on occasion when we bumped into each other at his events.

Anyone who has achieved a modicum of success or greatness in their life has done so a result of having stood on the shoulders of giants. I wish to acknowledge and thank those who have inspired and encouraged me over the years, the greatest of whom is my Mom.

Asset Protection Services of America

The inverted "V" displayed on our shield is the uppercase letter "L" in ancient Greek identifying the people of Lacedaemonia, which in historical times was the proper name for the Spartan state. The Greek cry "Molõn Labé" means "Come and Get Them" as spoken by King Leonidas in response to the Persian army's demand for the outnumbered Spartans (300 against 300,000) to surrender their weapons during battle in the narrow pass or 'hot gates' of Thermopylae in 480 B.C. The iconic expression has become a symbol of courage to defend that which belongs to you, even if faced against overwhelming or insurmountable odds.

Author

Jay Butler is the Managing Director of Asset Protection Services of America, the former Managing Director of Asset Protection Services International, Ltd and the former Vice-President of Sales and Marketing for Corporate Support Services of Nevada Inc. Mr. Butler holds a Bachelor's Degree of Fine Arts from Boston University.

Jay has provided customized business entity structuring for clients in all 50 states along with some of the most respected names in the industry including the Jay Mitton organization "the father of asset protection" and Real Estate Investor Association seminars.

While working with Wealth Protection Concepts, LLC under the tutelage of the former Las Vegas and North Las Vegas city attorney Carl E. Lovell Jr. (now deceased from Leukemia), Mr. Butler was bestowed the title of "Asset Protection Planner" for his competency and experience. He also co-authored the first edition of his book "Cover Your Assets: Legal Authorities on Asset Protection, Tax Strategies and Estate Planning" © 2006 with Dr. Lovell.

While residing in Switzerland, Mr. Butler was the Associate Director of "CO-Handelszentrum GmbH" providing Swiss company formation and administration services and executed a full-range of fiduciary responsibilities including sales, client support and international corporate compliance services (KYC, FATCA, AML, FATF and Swiss Code of Obligations).

Jay builds his relationships through consistent attention to detail and reliable support. He has traveled extensively throughout the United States (having visited 49 of the 50 states), explored 36 nations worldwide, and has lived in a total of 7 countries throughout North America, Central America, the Middle East, North Africa and Europe.

Dr Robert Hagopian is semi-retired and the former CEO of Nevada Trustee Services Group Inc, which has provided trustee services to attorneys and law firms throughout the United States since 2005, and the former CEO of the Commerce Bank Ltd in Hong Kong.

Since 1968, Robert has traveled extensively throughout Asia and lived in Japan, Hong Kong and the Philippines with current residency and offices in Manilla.

Dr. Hagopian holds a Bachelor of Science (BS) degree in business administration, an MsD (doctorate) in philosophy and a "jure Dignitatis" Bachelor of Laws degree.

Since 1984, Dr. Hagopian has been structuring business entities for optimum wealth preservation, profitability, asset protection and limiting personal liability through the use of domestic corporations, limited liability companies and various trust vehicles.

Robert has developed innovative processes for the acquisition, holding and marketing of real property. In 2008, Dr. Hagopian applied for the patent-pending "Equity Recovery Program". Based on IRC 351 rules for the transference of real estate to a corporation, the program lawfully avoids capital gains tax, self-employment and state taxes upon the sale of real property.

Contact Us

Please browse our website at www.AssetProtectionServices.com and contact us to schedule your free private asset protection consultation. We welcome the opportunity to hold a 3-way conference call with your tax advisor and/or legal counsel to address any specific questions or concerns you may have. Experience has demonstrated it favorable to have all related parties "on the same page" when creating your structure.

Asset Protection Services of America
701 South Carson Street (Suite #200)
Carson City, Nevada 89701-5239
Office   (775) 461-5255
Skype   Jay_Butler
E-Mail   info@AssetProtectionServices.com
Website   www.AssetProtectionServices.com

Books by Jay Butler
and Dr. Robert Hagopian

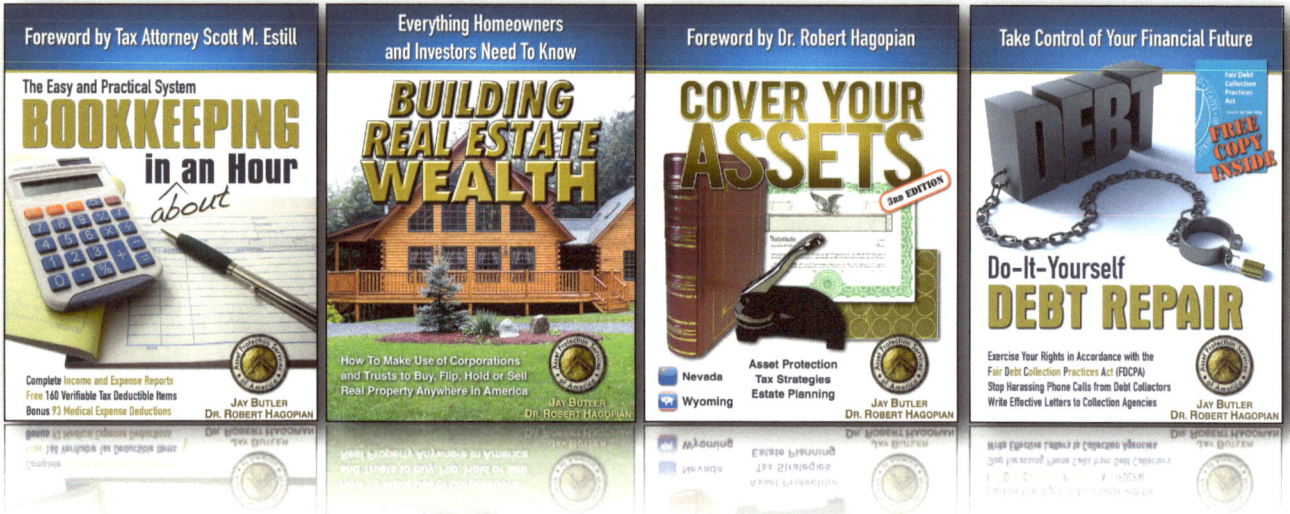

Bookkeeping in About an Hour ISBN 978-0-9914644-0-1
Building Real Estate Wealth ISBN 978-0-9914644-1-8
Cover Your Assets (3rd Edition) ISBN 978-0-9914644-2-5
Do-It-Yourself Debt Repair ISBN 978-0-9914644-7-0

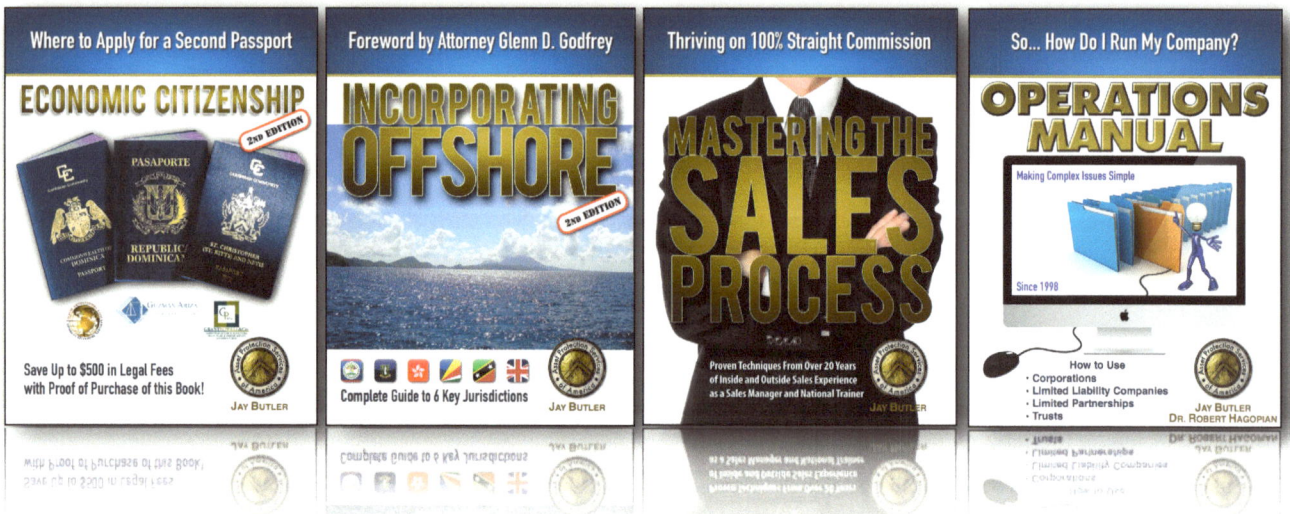

Economic Citizenship (2nd Edition) ISBN 978-0-9914644-4-9
Incorporating Offshore (2nd Edition) ISBN 978-0-9914644-5-6
Mastering the Sales Process ISBN 978-0-9914644-6-3
Operations Manual ISBN 978-0-9914644-3-2

Foreword

Not everyone is a successful salesperson. It takes perseverance, tenacity and a unique ability to manage your attitude. Over the past 34 years in my career as a regional sales manager for one of the largest sign companies in the world, I have hired and trained literally thousands of individuals. Some of those people whom I have hired and trained were promoted to begin regions of their own and have remained within the company for decades.

Those who have made it within the sales industry have done so because of their never ending commitment to self-improvement. And after reading many, many sales books over the years to continually improve my own attitude, work habits and sales skills, finally there is a book which concisely captures the essence of these techniques. *Mastering the Sales Process* is a must read for anyone wishing to improve their overall sales performance.

As an active salesman and sales manager for over 3 decades, I am in a unique position to speak to the qualities and attributes found in the best sales people. Jay Butler is one of the finest sales professionals I have ever met because he has mastered these techniques to the point that they have become part of his nature. Jay's personal performance within our company was consistent month in and month out. His leadership in the field and dedication to those around him led our region to producing award winning results year in and year out.

In this book *Mastering the Sales Process*, Jay shares the wisdom and knowledge he has learned throughout his sales career and as a national sales trainer to encourage and inspire others to achieve unlimited success. I highly recommend that anyone wanting to improve upon their sales read Jay's book and learn how these techniques can inspire greatness.

- Brian Kornuth
Regional Salesman and Sales Manager of 34 Years
Denver, Colorado

SIGNTRONIX

Signtronix.com
Authorized Dealer
District Manager
Regional Manager
National Sales Trainer

Jay Butler's Career with Signtronix

#3 National Salesman of the Year - 1998
#1 Regional Salesman of the Year - 1997, 1998, 1999, 2000, 2002, 2003
#1 National District Manager of the Year - 1998
#1 Regional District of the Year - 1997, 1998, 1999, 2000, 2002, 2003
#1 National Regional Office of the Year - 1998, 2000, 2003
#2 National Regional Office of the Year - 1997, 1999, 2002

What Are You Selling?

If you're a real estate agent, you're not selling homes and properties are not your business. If a car salesman, you're not selling automobiles and transportation is not your industry. If a chef, you're not selling food and neither the culinary arts nor hospitality are your occupation.

PEOPLE are your products and *EMOTIONS* are what you are sell!

Understanding the common denominator in all sales (which is people) and that which they purchase (perceived emotions) is the key to mastering the sales process. Do you think this philosophy is incorrect? Think again! Advertisers spend *billions* selling emotions to people:

"Oh-oh-oh Toyota, what a *feeling*"

"Mazda, it just *feels* right"

"Catch the Pepsi *spirit*"

"Open *happiness*, have a Coke and a *smile*"

"Sometimes you *feel* like a nut, sometimes you don't" - Almond Joy and Mounds

"Get the *sensation*" - York Peppermint Patty

"Double your *pleasure*, double your *fun*" - Double-mint Gum

"*Tastes* as good as it *smells*" Maxwell Coffee House

"Reach out, reach out and *touch* someone" - AT&T

"We *love* to fly and it *shows*" - Delta Airlines

"Never *follow*" - Audi

"We build *excitement*" - Pontiac

"Drive *safely*" - Volvo

"Like a *rock*" - Prudential

"The power to help you *succeed*" Pacific Life Insurance

Personality Types

The products or services you sell provide the means through which a person can access the emotions they value most. For example, if you sell fitness memberships at gym, you are not selling access to free-weights or aerobics classes but the means by which a person can feel better about themselves and their relationship with others. If you don't understand the four primary personality types, you will struggle tremendously in your ability to 'sell' the products your company represents and the perceived emotions your customers are seeking to 'buy'. In short, regardless of what (emotions) you are selling, your product (people) remains the same. To master the sales process, you simply must come to know and understand *people*.

Most people have heard of the "**Golden Rule**" which states,
"Do unto others as you would have them do unto you."

Few people have heard of the "**Rainbow Rule**" which states,
"Do unto others as *they* would have you do unto them!"

The difference is the person with whom the focus of the rule lies. Are you thinking about how to meet your client's needs based on your own values or theirs? In order to effectively communicate with yourself and other people, you must understand the four personality types.

Hippocrates	Astrology	Dr. Carl Yung
Blood	Air	Feeler
Phlegm	Earth	Sensor
Black Bowel	Water	Thinker
Yellow Bowel	Fire	Intuitor

Florence Litier	VALS Stanford	Flex Communicator
Phlegmatic	Belonger	Supporter
Sanguine	Emulator	Promoter
Melancholy	Achiever	Analyzer
Chloric	Social (A&B)	Controller

Animals	Automobiles	Foods	Shapes
Koala	Mini Van	Apple Pie	Circle
Monkey	Jeep	Pizza	Squiggle
Owl	Volvo	Broccoli	Square
Lion	Ferrari	Sushi	Triangle

Although knowledge of the four personality types dates back to the time of Hippocrates, schools do not adequately teach children how to communicate with themselves or others.

What Color are You?
65 - 85% of the Population is Different than You!

Instructions
Place an "x" where you are most "Open" or "Self-Contained" and "In-Direct" or "Direct"

Do you share your feelings freely in public?
Do you make decisions based on gut feelings?
Are you warm and relaxed?
Are you opinion and feeling oriented?
Are you flexible with your time with other people?

Open

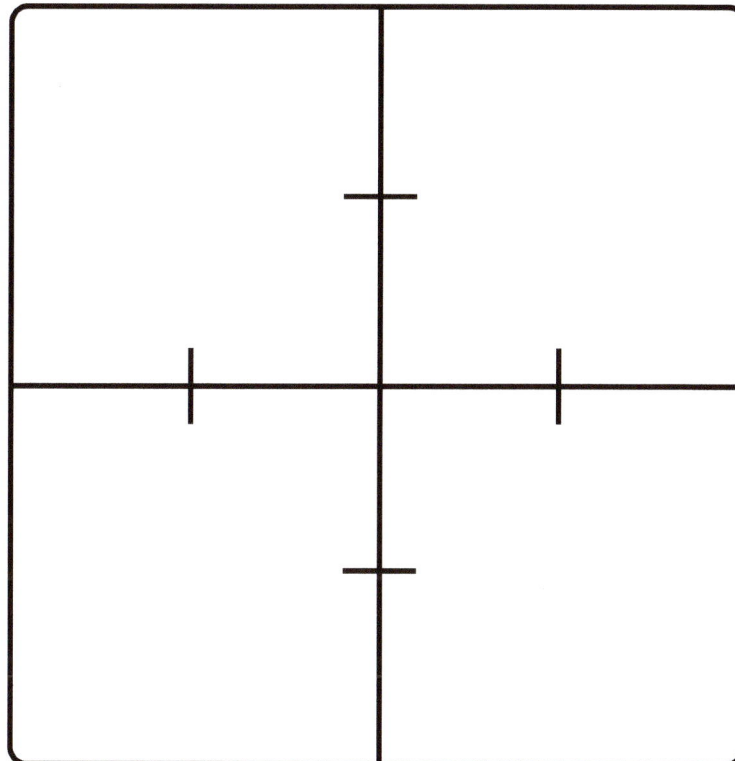

In-Direct

Do you approach change, decision and risk slowly and cautiously?

When in a group, are you laid-back and easy-going?

Direct

Do you approach change, decision and risk quickly & spontaneously?

When in a group, are you animated and out-going?

Self-Contained

Do you keep your feelings to yourself in public?
Do you make decisions based on evidence and logic?
Are you formal and proper?
Are you fact and task oriented?
Do you stick to the project at hand?

COLOR CHART

What is Your Primary Color?

You share your feelings freely in public
You make decisions based on gut feelings
You are warm and relaxed
You are opinion and feeling oriented
You are flexible with your time with other people

Open

35%

15%

In-Direct

Establish Friendships - Together! Supporters Avoid Confrontations Family Oriented (Picnics, etc) Like to Get to Know You Share - Help - Team - Environment Teachers, Counselors, Nurturers Allow People to Walk Over Them Warm, Big Smiles, Enjoy Hugs Great Lovers! Very Sensitive Drive Comfortable Cars	Like to Have Fun! Promoters Avoid Anything Boring Expressive and Charming Like Recognition Disorganized in an Organized Way Travel Agents, Sales People Love to Laugh, Tell Jokes Always Moving Around, Busy Great Story Tellers, Animated Drive Fast, Sporty Cars
I'm Right! Analyzers Hate to be Wrong Detail and Fact Oriented Like Things to Be Perfect Good Event Planners, Follow Thru Accountants, Scientists, Computer Paralysis by Analysis Time Conscientious Possessions Function Oriented Drive Economical Cars	I Won! Controllers Hate to Lose Anything Task Oriented, Focus on Business Like to Get Things Done Competitive Workaholics CEO, Presidents, Business Owner Will Never Cry in Public Fluff, Fluff, Slam Challenge and Money Motivated Drive High Performance Cars

Direct

You approach change, decision and risk slowly and cautiously

When in a group, you are laid-back and easy-going

You approach change, decision and risk quickly & spontaneously

When in a group, you are animated and out-going

35%

15%

Self-Contained

You keep your feelings to yourself in public
You make decisions based on evidence and logic
You are formal and proper
You are fact and task oriented
You stick to the project at hand

YELLOW

Behavior Pattern	Open and In-Direct
Priority	Relationships and Communication
Pace	Slow and Relaxed
Right - Left Brain	Predominately right-brained, but they can do a good job tapping into the left-side of the brain hemisphere which is why they tend to have the easiest time getting along with the other colors.
% of Population	35%
Strengths	Easy to get along with. Great listeners, which is one reason why they tend to have a lot of friends. They are team players, very loyal and dedicated. They avoid conflict and are very cooperative, which tends to give them a peaceful demeanor. They are non-threatening, love to help, and the most patient of all the personality types. They are extremely nurturing and supportive. They are known to be the best lovers in relation to quality.
Weaknesses	They have a tendency to be overly sensitive and take things personally, such as rejection for example. They tend to watch things happen instead of making them happen. They conform with the crowd because they don't want to 'rock the boat'. The more unassertive are often used by others. They are not as goal-oriented and tend to go-with-the-flow. It is easier for them to buy into other people's excuses. If a customer where to say "I can't afford to buy your product or services because I'm broke", they might respond by saying "That's ok, I'll just stop back by in a few months when things aren't so tight. Maybe then we'll be able to go to that pot-luck dinner together like we talked about."
Excited By	Tranquility, Stability and Harmony
Fears	Sudden Changes
Likes	Peace, love, happiness and animals. They would love harmony among nature and mankind. They like volunteering for things, helping and giving to others - especially the needy. They are most likely the ones to give money to people collecting money on street corners. They like to get to know people. They like to watch sunsets over the ocean.
Dislikes	Confrontation. Pushy and aggressive people, especially bullies, really irritate them. Loud or obnoxious people are a turn-off. They don't like to be pushed around, although it tends to happen quite a bit because they would rather submit to others than confront them. There is a threshold point where they will snap and become aggressive if pushed too far. They don't like people destroying rain forests, killing animals or causing wars.
Motivated By	Being Together and in Harmony
Save Them	Conflict and Risk
Want to Be	Accepted
Want You to Be	Pleasant
Motto	"Let's be friends and work together as a team so we can be one big family!"

BLUE

Behavior Pattern	Open and Direct
Priority	Relationships and Interacting
Pace	Fast and Spontaneous
Right - Left Brain	Predominately right-brained, more so than all the other types, which is why they tend to be very creative.
% of Population	15%
Strengths	Enthusiastic, optimistic, persuasive, playful, charming, motivating, bubbly, funny, refreshing, convincing and animated. They are creative and highly intuitive because of the dominant use of the right hemisphere of the brain. They are usually the life of the party, love to socialize with people, and are excellent promoters. They are known to be the best lovers in regard to variety and are also very flirtatious.
Weaknesses	Generally speaking, they are generally speaking. In other words, they tend to talk too much and, on top of that, they tend to talk before thinking. They are known to open their mouths when they wake up and don't close them until they go to sleep. They are disorganized, but in an organized fashion. They tend to be the poorest savers of all the colors. Their idea of checking the balance in their check books is to see if they have any more checks. If there are more checks, there must be more money! They are poor on follow-up, tend to be forgetful and are known to be a bit scatter-brained. They are likely to go off on five different subjects or angles within the same five minute conversation. They have a tendency to exaggerate and come across as evasive or even phony.
Excited By	Action and Being Free to Be Creative
Fears	Not Being Liked
Likes	They like to have fun! Their attitude is, "if it's not fun, why do it?" They like to get recognition and enjoy testimonials because they love to be in the spotlight. They like to party and have a good time. They want to know that you like them. They like to get the big picture rather than the technical details. They like excitement and they like to dream.
Dislikes	They don't like anything that's boring. They don't like too much technical, detailed or logical stuff. They don't like anything or anyone that tries to take away their fun. They don't like being alone. They don't like rigid systems, extensive rules or long drawn-out processes.
Motivated By	Fun and Being Part of the Chase
Save Them	Monotonous Effort
Want to Be	Noticed and Admired
Want You to Be	Fun and Exciting
Motto	"Hey, let me tell you a joke and then after that I'll tell you another one!"

GREEN

Behavior Pattern	Self-Contained and In-Direct
Priority	Tasks and Facts
Pace	Slow and Systematic
Right - Left Brain	Predominately left-brained more than all the other types, which is why they are very factual and analytically oriented.
% of Population	35%
Strengths	They are accurate, precise, efficient, well-read, conscientious, dependable and the most organized of all the colors. They have great follow-through skills and good at persisting through tasks that most would consider boring. They are good problem solvers and tend to be very neat. They are great planners and once they commit, they will consistently work their plans. They are the best lovers in relation to appropriateness.
Weaknesses	Paralysis by analysis. Too critical and overly cautious. Hard to please because they are perfectionists. Easily depressed because most people and situations don't meet their stringent standards. They tend to be more pessimistic and skeptical than the other colors. They can be withdrawn from others and tend be loners. They will spend lots of quiet time seeking revenge from those who have performed wrong doings to them.
Excited By	Logic and Reason
Fears	Being Illogical and Irrational
Likes	Details, facts, analyzing, figuring things out, taking things apart. They like being on time, being right, being accurate and being precise. They like organization and scheduling things. They like processes and systems, order and structure, planning and preparing. They like things to be in a perfect line and prefer things stay in the box. They like time and predictability as there is a time and place for everything.
Dislikes	Being wrong, disorganization, obnoxious people, pushy people or people who are not on time. They don't like people who are not precise or prepared. They don't like spontaneity or surprises.
Motivated By	Detailed Processes and Sophisticated Systems
Save Them	From Being Wrong or Embarrassed
Want to Be	Right
Want You to Be	Prepared and Precise
Motto	"Documentation beats conversation, therefore may I please see the facts?"

RED

Behavior Pattern	Self-Contained and Direct
Priority	Tasks and Facts
Pace	Fast and Decisive
Right - Left Brain	Predominately left-brained and easily able to tap into the right also.
% of Population	15%
Strengths	These are the people we call our 'natural born leaders'. They tend to portray the most confidence of all the colors. They are powerful and take massive action toward their goals. They are driven, goal-oriented, risk takers and thrive on opposition. They are independent and self-sufficient. They are dynamic individuals with lots of energy. They can successfully juggle many tasks at the same time and tend to make the quickest decisions once they've had a chance to gather and review the appropriate information. They are the best lovers in relation to quantity.
Weaknesses	Even though they make decisions quickly, they have a tendency to wait until the pressure builds up before taking action to complete the goal. In other words they have a tendency to procrastinate at times. They are the most unsympathetic of all the colors and have the tendency to forget that other people have feelings. They are impatient. They can come off as rude and pushy brats. They like to argue, although they would prefer to call it a debate. They are usually the most stubborn and unteachable of all the colors because they feel that they know it all. They have short tempers. They tend to be too domineering and they don't listen well.
Excited By	Action, Action and More Action
Fears	Being Hustled and Being Soft
Likes	They like a challenge. They like talking about their credentials and how important they are. They like to know that you are important and you are connected with the 'important' people. They like, no they love, being in control. They like power. They tend to like stress and work better under stress than the other colors. They like to argue and they like to win. They like to be in charge and to lead. They like doing things that make money.
Dislikes	They don't like small talk or wasting their time. They don't like being behind or following others. They don't like feeling like they are missing something because they want to be on top of everything. They don't like to stop and smell the roses, but if they do they will count the number of roses they smelled and ask you how many you smelled for the day. They don't like to get too mushy or too touchy-feely in public. They don't cry.
Motivated By	Being #1, Being the Best, Winning, Accomplishment
Save Them	Time
Want to Be	In Control
Want You to Be	Blunt and to the Point
Motto	"I've already won, so don't even bother following me - you won't make it."

Interacting with People

Have you ever noticed that people like to do business with people they like? Birds of a feather, flock together. People want to do business with other people who are just like them and whose company they enjoy. How many examples can you find in the following two illustrations that demonstrate the various personality types and methods of communication?

Mr Blue *(Visual)* and Miss Green *(Auditory)*

Blue   "Isn't this the most exciting cell phone product you've ever seen?"

Green   "I suppose, but I wanted to hear more about the new 2013 comparison between your company's model 'abc' and the competitor's model 'xyz'."

Blue   "Well, our 'abc' model is guaranteed 'fun in a box'. Our competitor's model 'xyz' has got to be the most boring invention to date; why you could hardly even call it an invention. In fact, we had one client recently who tried to place a video call --"

Green   "I just need to listen to more details about the compatibility with various operating systems, its power supply specifications and accessory availability."

Blue   "Wow, that's an information overload to me. I'm just trying to paint you a big picture on all the possibilities of how this video phone can help you make new friends!"

Green   "You'll have to tone-it down sir, I don't resonate with what you're saying."

Blue   "Oh, I see."

Green   "I have 7.5 more minutes before I must begin preparing for my next scheduled appointment. So if you are going to provide me with a detailed description of the phone's energy consumption options then I'm all ears."

Blue   "You mean, what's the power source?"

Green   "Why yes! What are the alternating current requirements of your 2013 model 'abc' with special attachments that come with a 2 year unlimited warranty?"

Blue   "It runs on 110 or 220 volts and you can plug it into the wall or use batteries."

Green   "Clearly that was designed by an engineer with my international needs in mind. I'd like two units shipped to my home address by way of express delivery please."

Dr Red *(Visual)* and Mrs Yellow *(Kinesthetic)*

Red "Yes, that pre-owned vehicle is in perfect condition. Come on into my office so that we can take a look at look the prices for you. Watch your step now . . ."

Yellow "Thank you. Oh how delightful, is this a photo of you and your brother fishing?"

Red "Yes, I caught 8 shiny trout that day. My little brother only caught 7."

Yellow "Ahhh . . . Summers are such a wonderful time to spend together with family and friends at outdoor picnics."

Red "Right. I invested in a highly regarded outdoor training survival course, headed by the regional champion at the time, to learn vital skills and techniques on foresting, food preparedness and medical emergencies."

Yellow "How I just love tranquil forests! All of the pretty trees, fragrant flowers and cute little animals living harmoniously together. If only our local communities were so peaceful and followed the example of nature."

Red "He just wanted to be right in saying he would catch more fish than me that day, but in the end - I won! Well, back to business. I'm sure your children will be in good hands with this state-of-the-art minivan."

Yellow "Oh yes, I do like the color and the heated seats are so warm and comfortable."

Red "Where do you picture yourself driving it tonight?"

Yellow "I would love to pick my son up from soccer and take all his friends out for pizza. We'll all have such a great time together!"

Red "Excellent. Well, I don't want to be pushy or anything but --"

Yellow "Oh no, I don't like pushy people."

Red "And yet there is no time like the present. What did you say your address was?"

Yellow "Oh, 456 Anywhere Lane. Does this mean I get to take it home?"

Red "Why of course, that's why we're here - to help you see your dreams come true!"

Methods of Communication

As humans, we experience this life through our bodies. Our five primary senses are that of sight, sound, emotion, taste and smell. The technical terms for such perceptions of reality are visual, auditory, kinesthetic, gustatory and olfactory. Given that we do not predominately go through life sniffing and licking things (much like a K-9 or squirrel), we rely on our ability to see, hear and feel to interact in this world.

If you desire to master the sales process and effectively communicate with yourself and others, you must understand the methods of communication through we which we transmit information to one another daily. For example, numerous psychological studies have found and concurred that when communicating people rely on the following:

55% - Physiology
38% - Tone of Voice
7% - Word Choice

Physiology is a word used to describe your 'body language'. The manner in which you use your body while communicating constitutes a full 55% of the meaning conveyed during a conversation. We have all heard the phrase "It's not what you say, but how you say it". This lends to the notion that people place more than a third of the value of what you say (38%) on *how* you say it. Lastly, our choice of words weighs in at a mere 7% in value in comparison to our body language and tone of voice. Unfortunately, far too many people are looking for the right things to say and have placed too high an opinion on sales scripts. "You cannot say the wrong thing to the right person, and you cannot say the right thing to the wrong person". Although using proper terminology is of great help in closing a higher percentage of business, it pales in comparison to understanding how to effectively make use of the three primary methods of communication to avail the power of persuasion and hold influence over others.

Visual Communications

Visual

Distinctions

Head	Vertical
Eyes	Looking Upward
Shoulders	Up and Back
Breathing	High in the Chest
Comfort Zone	Large
Body Language	Fast and Animated
Speech	Specific, Rapid, Loud
Motto	'Show Me' Your Products or Services

Sub-Modalities

Brightness	Dimension	Hue	Panorama	Saturation	Speed
Color	Direction	Location	Participatory	Shade	Vibrant
Clarity	Focus	Motion	Proximity	Size	Viewpoint

Predicate Words

Appear	Dawn	Focused	Illuminate	Reveal	Sparkling
Brilliant	Enlighten	Foggy	Look	See	Sunny
Clear	Envision	Hazy	Panorama	Sharp	Twinkle
Crystal	Flash	Imagine	Picture	Show	View

Predicate Phrases

An eyeful	Horse of a different color	Plainly see
Appears to me	In light of	Pretty as a picture
A shadow of a doubt	In person	See to it
Bird's eye view	In view of	Short Sighted
Catch a glimpse of	Looks like	Showing off
Clear Cut	Makes a scene	Sight for sore eyes
Dim View	Mental image	Staring off into space
Eye to eye	Mental picture	Take a peek
Flashed on	Mind's eye	Tunnel vision
Get a perspective on	Naked eye	Under your nose
Get a scope on	Paint a picture	Up front
Hazy idea	Photographic memory	Well defined

Auditory Communications

Distinctions

Head	Angled
Eyes	Looking to the Side(s)
Shoulders	Loose and Easy
Breathing	Relaxed and Centered
Comfort Zone	Medium and Polite
Body Language	Fluid Body Motions
Speech	Musical Language Patterns
Motto	'Tell Me' About Your Products or Services

Sub-Modalities

Cadence	Duration	Harmony	Pitch	Rhythm	Timbre
Digital	Echo	Inflection	Resonance	Stereo	Tone
Direction	Feedback	Location	Reverberation	Tempo	Volume

Predicate Words

All-ears	Deaf	Harmonize	Mellifluous	Resonate	Sounds
Attune	Dissonance	Listen	Overtones	Rings a Bell	Tune In / Out
Come-again	Hear	Make Music	Question	Silence	Unhearing

Predicate Phrases

Afterthought	Hidden message	Rings a bell
Blabbermouth	Hold your tongue	State your purpose
Clear as a bell	Idle talk	Tattletale
Clearly expressed	Inquire into	To tell the truth
Call on	Keynote speaker	Tongue-tied
Describe in detail	Loud and clear	Tuned in / Tuned out
Earful	Manner of speaking	Unheard of
Express Yourself	Pay attention to	Utterly
Give an account of	Power of speech	Voice an opinion
Give me your ear	Purrs like a kitten	Well informed
Grant an audience	Outspoken	Within hearing range
Heard voices	Rap session	Word for word

Kinesthetic Communications

Distinctions

Head	Angled and Down
Eyes	Looking Down and Right
Shoulders	Forward and Down
Breathing	Deep and Meaningful
Comfort Zone	Small and Reserved
Body Language	Tight and Cautious
Speech	Slow and Articulate
Motto	'Experience' Your Products or Services

Sub-Modalities

Breathing	Form	Moisture	Rigidity	Size	Texture
Direction	Intensity	Movement	Sensation	Temperature	Vibration
Distance	Location	Pressure	Shape	Tension	Weight

Predicate Words

Burn	Crazy	Hard	Slip	Throw	Unfeeling
Catch	Feel	Hold	Solid	Tight	Unyielding
Concrete	Grasp	Scrape	Suffer	Touch	Veiled
Contact	Handle	Slide	Tap	Turn	Weigh

Predicate Phrases

All washed up	Get your goat	Pain in the neck
Boils down to	Hand in hand	Pull some strings
Chip off the old block	Hang in there	Sharp as a tack
Come to grips with	Heated argument	Slipped my mind
Control yourself	Hold it	Smooth operator
Calm, cool and collected	Hot-headed	So-so
Firm foundations	Keep your shirt on	Start from scratch
Floating on thin air	Know-how	Stiff upper lip
Get a handle on it	Lay your cards on the table	Stuffed Shirt
Get a load of this	Light-headed	Too much of a hassle
Get in touch with	Moment of panic	Topsy-turvy
Get the drift of	Not following you	Underhanded

Eye Accessing Cues

Our brains have an unlimited capacity to learn and retain information. How may languages do you want to learn? How many instruments do you want to play? As many as you desire! However, memory without the ability to recall the information serves little purpose.

Our minds are wired in a manner similar to that of a computer operating system. Most "start" or "finder" files are located on the bottom left-hand corner of the monitor. Just as a mouse is used to access the hard drive of your computer, so too can you access memories, data and creativity in your mind through the movement of your eyes. Don't think it will work? Try it!

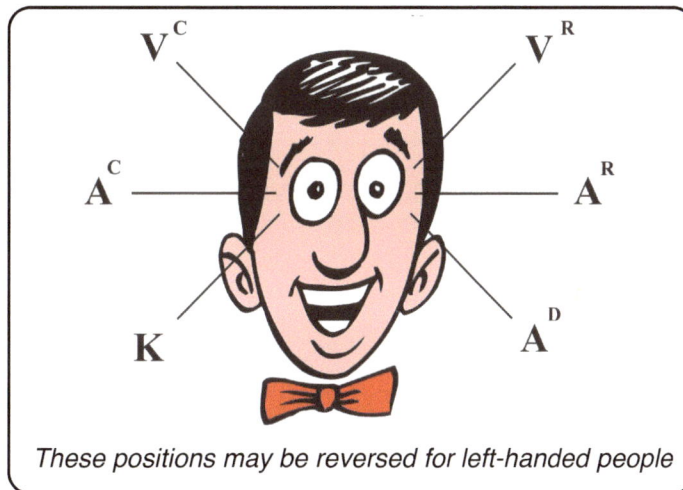

These positions may be reversed for left-handed people

VR	*Visual Recall*	Seeing images of things seen before in the way they were before. *"What color are your mother's eyes?" "What color is your coat?"*
VC	*Visual Constructed*	Seeing images of things differently or never before visualized. *"What would you look like from the other side of the room?"*
AR	*Auditory Recall*	Remembering sounds heard before. *"What does the alarm on your clock sound like?"*
AC	*Auditory Constructed*	Putting words, sounds or phrases together in a new way. *"Imagine a siren sound made by an electric guitar."*
AD	Auditory Digital	Talking to oneself. *"Do you remember reciting the pledge of allegiance?"*
K	Kinesthetic	Emotions, tactile (touch) and proprioceptive (muscle) sensations. *"What is the feeling of touching a pine cone?"*

The Introduction

If you've heard the saying "you never have a second chance to make a first impression", then perhaps you should be asking yourself if you are making the best use of this knowledge.

Do all the little things that, when combined, compound and make a big difference in how people perceive you. For example, are you well-groomed? Do you dress appropriately? Does your breath smell? Are you clean shaven? Are you well-rested on a regular basis?

> Hi! I was wondering if you could help me?
>
> My name is . . .

You are selling to *people* and they are purchasing the (perceived) emotions they believe *you* have to offer through your products or services. Statistics show that people arrive at a pre-conceived notion of who they think you are within thirty seconds of meeting you. Do **not** try and 'sell them' in your intro. Make the most of your brief introduction by having confidence, patience, positive energy and a relaxing smile!

Formal Introduction

1.) Who are you? *(State your full name slowly and clearly)*
2.) Where do you work? *(Give your full company name)*

[Qualify to speak with the **Owners** of the business]

3.) What do you do? *(Provide a concise description)*
4.) Why are you here? *(Offer a simple explanation)*
5.) What do you want? *(Instruct them on what to do next)*

[Qualify to speak with any **Partners** in the business]

Immediate Objections

No Time I understand. I wasn't expecting you to be free now. When would be the best time for us to get together for just a few moments, in the mornings or evenings?

Partners I understand. I appreciate the fact that you make your business decisions together. When would be the best time for all of us to meet for just a few moments, during the beginning of the business week or toward the weekend?

No Interest I understand. Maybe you could help me in another way. Who do you know that might be interested in taking advantage of our products or services?

Asking Questions

If you find that people are not as receptive to you as you would like, then you may want to consider the quality of questions you are asking (yourself) and your clients on a consistent basis. Asking yourself questions is referred to as 'self-talk', asking questions of your clients is often referred to as 'inquiring', 'warming them up', or 'investigating'. Write down what you consider to be the top-five most important questions you need to be asking clients. Bear in mind, 'what type of response do you want to elicit from the client'.

Asking Open-Ended Questions

Incorrect	Correct
"I saw you responded to our advertisement recently, are you still interested in our listed products or services?"	"I saw you responded to our advertisement recently, which of our listed products or services caught your attention?"
"Did you have a chance to read through the materials we e-mailed you?"	"What did you like best about the materials we e-mailed you?"
"Do you want me to call you back?"	"When is the best time for me to reach you?"
"I don't know the answer to your inquiry, can you hold while I transfer you to someone who might be more knowledgable than me?"	"Let me research that and get back to you with an answer. Did you have any other concerns I could look into for you?"
"I believe our 'blank' product or service will work best for you. Do you know what 'color' you want?	"I believe our 'blank' product or service will work best for you. Would you prefer using our products or services in 'red' or 'blue'?
"How come you don't like our products or services?"	"How could our products or services better meet your needs?"
"Are you ready to place your order with us today?"	"How would you like to process your order with us today; cash, check or credit card?"
(Self-Talk) "Why won't this guy buy from me? What's his problem?"	(Self-Talk) "What do I need to provide this guy for him to buy from me? Where can I add more value to initiate his purchase?"

Questions to Avoid

‣ Avoid Questions to which a client can simply respond "No".
‣ Avoid Questions which are combative or negative in nature.
‣ Avoid Questions that pass responsibility on to others.

Questions to Ask

‣ Ask Questions which require the client to answer in a sentence.
‣ Ask Questions which build rapport and encourage the client.
‣ Ask Questions that show genuine concern and commitment.

1.) " _____
_____
_____
_____
_____
_____? "

2.) " _____
_____
_____
_____? "

3.) " _____
_____
_____
_____
_____? "

4.) " _____
_____
_____
_____
_____? "

5.) " _____
_____
_____
_____
_____? "

The Presentation

Sales presentations are as varied as there are products and services. However so structured, your presentation must be well engineered to capture the attention of all four personality types and communicate the information in a manner which appeals to all three primary methods of communication. You must not only memorize your presentation, you must *live* it. People are giving you a stage - bring them into your world and perform! Deliver your presentation with so much passion, enthusiasm and conviction clients will be delighted to buy from you.

Moving Away - Moving Toward

Some people 'move away' from what they don't want, while others 'move toward' what they do want. Include examples of what your products or services do and don't do.

"Our satellite technology gives you access to over 100 top-rated TV, Radio and Movie channels without any of those annoying commercial interruptions you get now."

Internally Motivated - Externally Motivated

Some people are 'internally motivated', while others are 'externally motivated'. Include examples of how your products or services will reward a client's own-decision and should be supported by their family, friends or local community.

"Our life insurance policies can cover all your family's future needs in the event of your untimely death. Should you suffer a fatal car accident or plane crash, your kids would still be able to attend college. Now who in their right mind would criticize you for doing that?"

Details - Chunking

Some people enjoy processing long series of information, steps or procedures, while others fair better 'chunking' information into easier concepts. Explain your products or services in a way which incorporates both types of learning styles.

"Our headsets utilize a proprietary encryption that takes the senders signal, scrambles each piece of voice data into over 256 bits of random code, transmits it through an FCC approved commercial wave length and then re-configures the data on the receiving end, all with outstanding clarity. It's better than using two styrofoam cups connected by a string!"

Facts Tell - Stories Sell

"Our extended road-side assistance program offers complete 24-hour emergency help."
"Do you want to explain to your wife why you don't have road-side assistance when you're stranded on the side of the road while she's going into labor?"

An Unfair Advantage

As a professional sales person, you have an unfair advantage over your clients in that you know the beginning of the sales presentation from the end and the end from the beginning. Such an unfair advantage includes your awareness of the client's concerns and objections before-hand. If you know where the potholes are on a road you've traveled frequently, don't you do your best to avoid them? Not only is it more comfortable for the passengers (your clients) but it also prevents your suspension from being worn out (your emotional well-being). Make it *easy* on your clients to buy from you and avoid creating any unnecessary objections.
You feel great when you have just sold your client a product or service! Keep that wonderful feeling (an unfair advantage) with you and draw on it the next time you make a 'cold call'. If your efforts are consistent and persistent, the person who answers may be your next sale!

Scripting Your Presentation

To maximize your effectiveness, you simply *must* write out your entire presentation word for word from beginning to end - *by hand*. Using a computer for this exercise will not do. The snail's pace at which you must write by hand will force you to consider the literal meaning and use of each word choice and *connect you* with the emotional, philosophical and spiritual aspects of your presentation. You will cheat no one other than yourself in failing to do this.

Adjusting Your Presentation

Adjusting your presentation is akin to manually finding and maintaining a good radio station. You can move the knob large distances at the beginning, but then you need to settle in on a format which gels with your personality and character. Just as radio signals fade in and out when traveling across town, so too do you need to be vigilant in keeping yourself 'tuned in' to your clients by making regular proactive micro-adjustments to your presentation.

Using Humor

Look for natural places in your presentation to laugh as doing so not only lightens the atmosphere, it helps keep you happy over time. There's nothing quite like having to deliver the same boring and repetitious presentation day in and day out and not enjoying it. Keep the experience light, fun, fresh and new - it's easier on your clients and you!

The Close

The 'close' is where you (finally) present your client with the prices for your products or services. A closing should last anywhere from 5 to 15 minutes or more depending on the nature of the products or services being sold. However, the close is not where you 'sell' per say, it is where you 'close' on what you should have already 'sold' in the eyes of the client. The closing is where sales people have the least amount of experience and the greatest amount of stress. It must therefore be the one area of your presentation where you invest a considerable amount of time and energy to perfect it.

One-Call Closers

Arguably the hardest form of selling is a 'one-call' close, which means you either sell to the client during your first (and only) visit or you do not. Professional one-call closers will *never* return a second-time to try to consummate a sale. Few people perfect this art of selling.

Multi-Close Sales

Without diminishing the difficulty in a multi-close sales environment, you have an opportunity to develop a professional relationship with the client and are granted time to find creative ways of building additional value in your products or services. Competition, current events, product availability, change in company direction, inaccurate information, transportation and poor communication all play a huge factor in the success of consummating a multi-close sale.

Organization and Precision

When you reach for your calculator you should know exactly where it is and it ought to be there. Laying out your close is much like a plane coming in for a landing, there is a very small window of opportunity for error. Life will grant you some wiggle room to maneuver, but if your close is not precise it will make for a very rough landing or possibly a spectacular crash.

Justifying Prices

The close is where you take the value you (should) have built during your presentation and align it to your prices. If your cost or 'price point' is not in alignment with your market, then you may have a very challenging time convincing your clients to conduct business with you. At the same time, be careful not to under-sell as the adage 'you get what you pay for' will inevitably come to your client's mind. Price justification is an on-going balancing act.

No = Know

Nobody wants to be at the mercy of a robot sales person who simply will not hear the word 'no'. However, it is important to understand that people must be taken through an information gathering process to 'know' enough information which meets their own internal rules and allow themselves to feel comfortable making a purchasing decision. This process generally requires 7 or 8 objections. To successfully navigate your way through this mental and emotional obstacle course, you need to listen carefully to what your clients are saying and hear what they are not telling you. When a client tells you "No, I'm not interested", in all likelihood, it means "I don't *know* why I should be interested in your products or services."

Promoting - Testimonials

When you promote yourself (or your company), you basically come across like this:
"We are the best and you need to trust us for no real reason other than because we say so."

When you harness the power of client testimonials, they come across on your behalf like this:
"You need to do business with this company because I had a great experience with them."

Your close should incorporate absolutely no less than three powerful, relevant and timely testimonials about how your products or services impacted their lives. You are *losing sales* if you do not consistently demonstrate, through the experience of others, why clients should be doing business with you. If you don't have any testimonials, start building them immediately.

Assume the Sale

We have all been someone else's client, have we not? Have you ever experienced what it is like to try to purchase a product or service from someone who is assuming you're *not* there to make a purchase? Not only is it uncomfortable, it's almost rude. You want to assume the sale. You should absolutely, unquestionably assume that your clients are there for no other reason than to purchase your products or services. Only questions like 'which size', 'what color' or 'how many' remain. Your purpose is to help uncover such desires, not the impetus.

Contract Close

Regardless of your product or service, you will invariably need to turn in paperwork to complete your order. So it's wise to 'begin with the end in mind' and pull those documents out while you are speaking with your client. If they are asking for the price (at an appropriate time), add it up for them on an invoice or order form, then pass them your pen and show them where to sign. Asking for their address is one of the easiest ways to get the paperwork going and alleviates a potentially uncomfortable moment when beginning to fill-out an order form.

A Business of Thirds

Experience has shown the sales industry to be a business of thirds. In general, you should be 'closing' one out of every three qualified prospects. If your numbers fall below this average it could be for a number of reasons but would most likely include one or more of the following:

‣ Aspects throughout your presentation are mediocre and you need to refine your skills.

‣ You are rushing or under stress and not adequately listening to your clients.

‣ You have become lackadaisical in the quantity of presentations given in a set period of time.

‣ Presenting to clients who aren't interested or qualified to purchase your product or services.

‣ Your close is weak; your testimonials lack credibility; you need to learn more closing stories.

‣ You have knowingly (or unknowingly) negatively changed portions of your presentation.

‣ The quality of your product or services has diminished or become comparatively expensive.

‣ You have lost your passion and enthusiasm for the work you once enjoyed performing.

Trusting the Numbers

Hearing a definitive 'no' from a client is emotionally difficult. In fact, dealing with the fear of rejection is one of the hardest parts of selling. Most people do not last long in the sales industry because of the emotional highs and lows. However, "when you change the way you look at things, the things you look at change". As you begin to track your performance, you may realize that you are selling, say, 1 out of every 8 presentations. Hearing the next seven no's isn't quite as painful because statistically you know you are due for a sale. But to have such certainty you absolutely, positively, must track your sales performance. If you feel this is unimportant for some reason, try and explain not following your stats to a sports professional. If you're unaware of your past performance, it is impossible to gauge what you are doing correctly or incorrectly and you'll be unable to plan or prepare for the future. So long as you stay 'on top of your game' you can trust the numbers and learn to love hearing 'no'.

Straight Commission vs. Base + Commission

In my 20+ year sales career, I have only worked a base + commission opportunity once, for a period of about 6 months, and I didn't care for it. I do understand those who elect a base + commission environment, particularly if you are new to the industry or are married and have children. However, the greatest opportunities for earnings will generally not be found in a base + commission environment. Straight commission sales enable you to have the freedom and responsibility to live your life as you choose. You have no one to blame for your failures, but no one can take away your pride and confidence when you reach new levels of success either. Fortune favors the bold. If you want the independence, the lifestyle, and the autonomy, then you have to claim the responsibility, the liability, and the risks inherent with straight commission opportunities. Once you experience 100% straight commission earnings, it is very difficult (if not impossible) to return to a base + commission job.

Emotional Levels

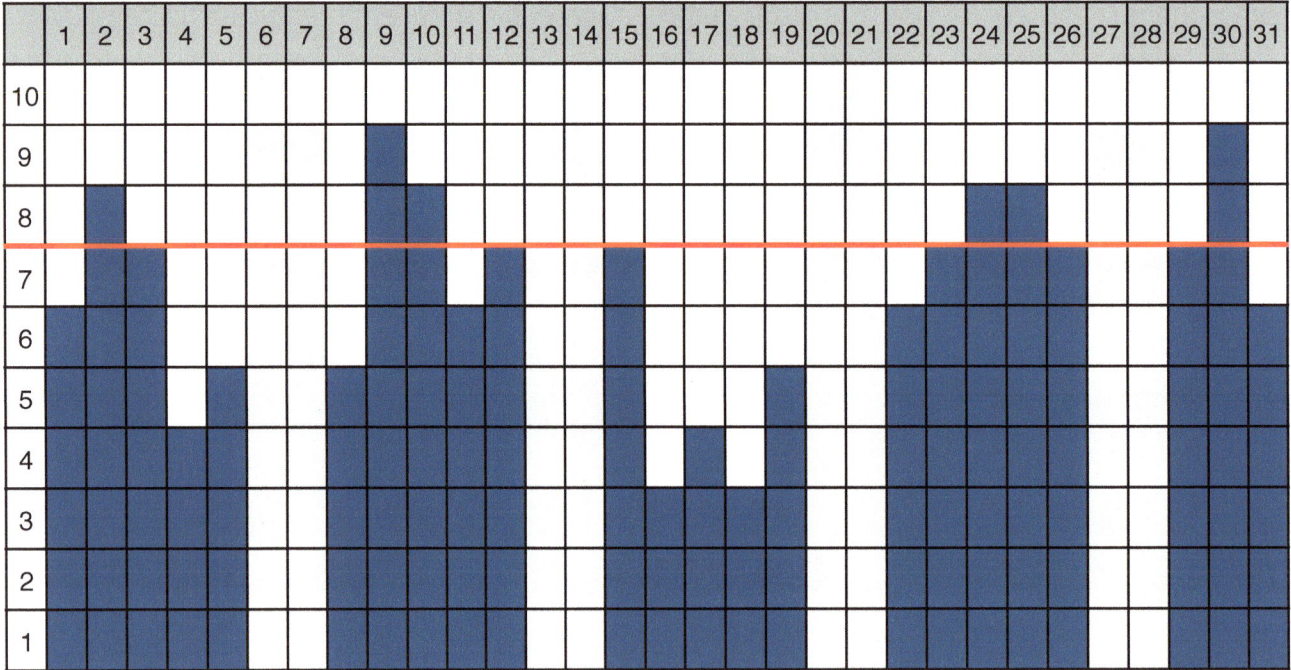

To enjoy long-term success in sales, you must 'discipline your disappointments' and prevent weekly emotional roller coasters (above). If you allow your mental well-being to be dictated by external events you will soon burn-out. To succeed, maintain a consistent state-of-mind which remains between an 8 out of 10 throughout every work-week in the month (below).

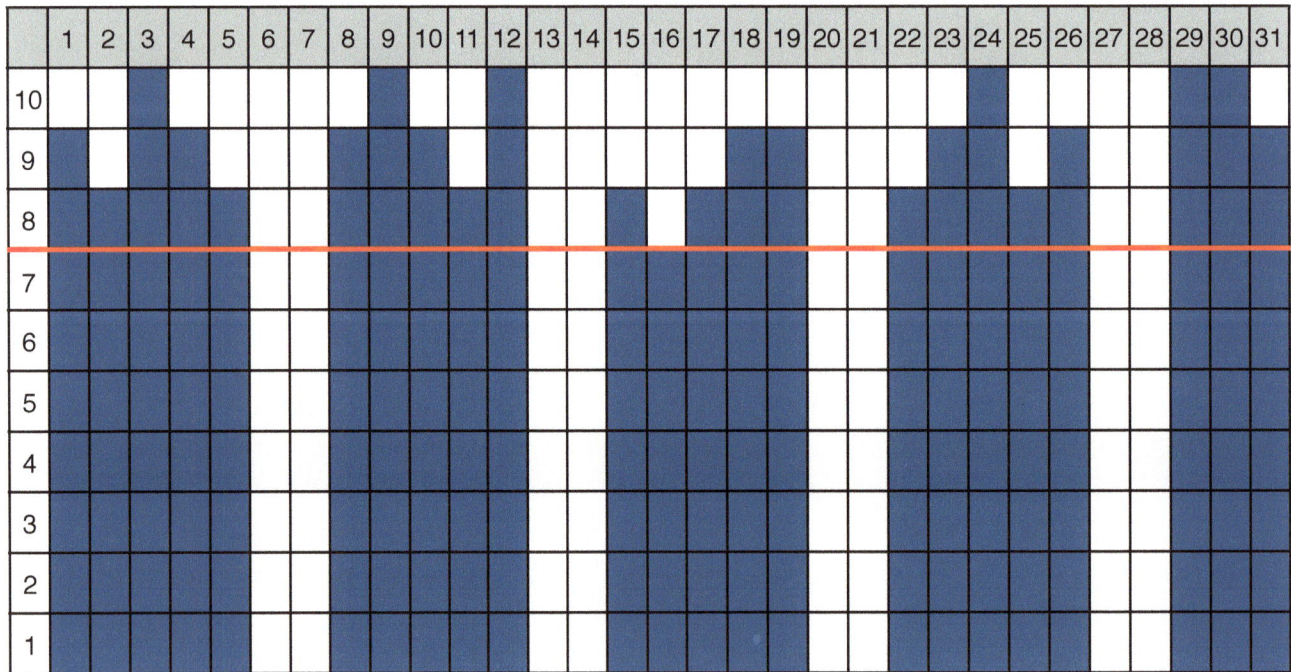

Overcoming Objections

What is an objection? Conceptually, I believe you may know the answer to this question. But specifically, do you really know what an objection is from a technical point of view?

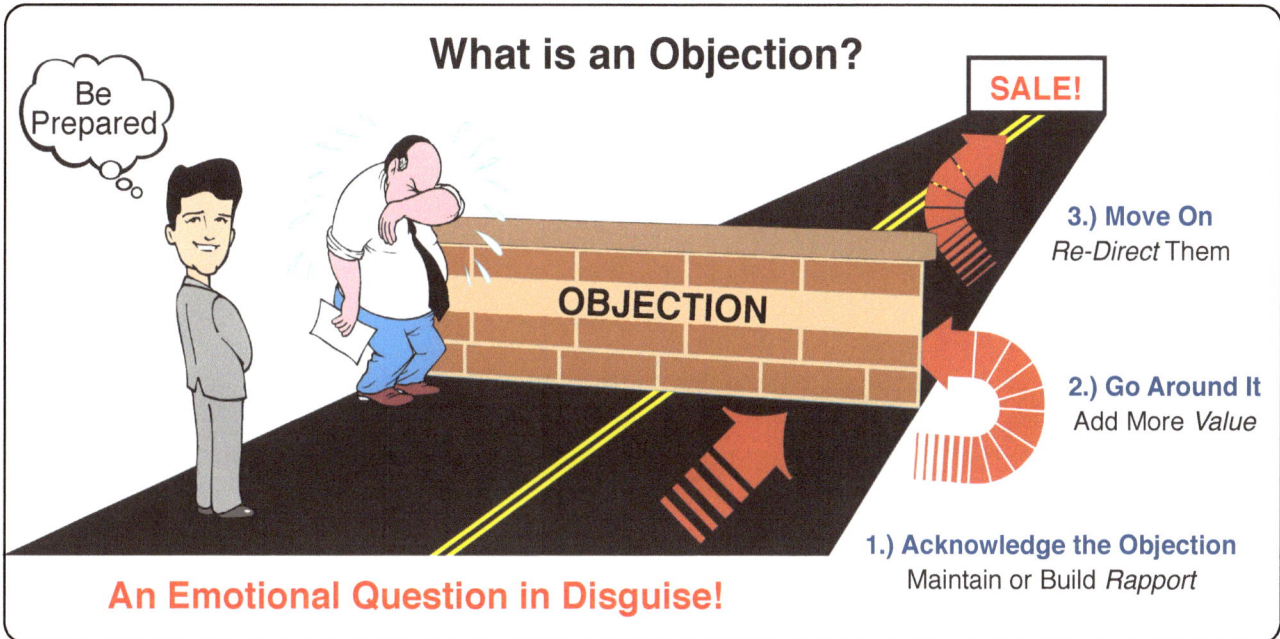

Your mission, should you choose to accept it, is to address the emotionally charged question in disguise that is an objection. Be prepared by writing down answers to the top five most frequently raised objections from your clients and review the answers regularly.

Objection

"Let's cut to the bottom-line here, how much do these things cost? What's the price?"

Questions

"Why should I *spend* my hard-earned money (or good credit) on your products or services?"
"Will your products or services genuinely give me the *results* I'm seeking?"
"Where is the *value* in all of this for me?"
"Why should I even bother spending my *time* to listen to you any further?"

Emotions

"I'm *concerned* that I'll buy your products or services from you and they won't work."
"I'm *scared* of someone trying to take advantage of me."
"I'm *torn* because I can't afford to lose anymore business."
"I'm *frustrated* because I don't know if I can *trust* you."

Answer

1.) Acknowledge the Objection
(Maintain or Build *Rapport*)

[Name of Client], I understand. (Smile and slowly nod your head up and down) I know exactly how you feel because I have been in your shoes wanting to know the same thing. "Show me the money!" Right? (Laugh gently) I'll tell you what (placing both your hands over your heart), I promise not to play any games with you, okay?

2.) Go Around It
(Add More *Value*)

(Open your arms and relax) The answer to your question honestly depends because we have over "x number" of products or services from which to choose. It's like asking "how much is a bag of groceries"? (Pause) It depends on what you put in the bag, right? (Smile and breath) We have . . . (Take your time to carefully and thoughtfully list at least three (3) products or services you offer along with their most important features and benefits)

3.) Move On
(*Re-Direct* Them)

Allow me to do three things for you please:

1.) I'd like to learn a little bit more about your business so that we can determine if you are even in need of our products or services. (Giving them an 'out' helps to reduce stress)
2.) Once we've learned how our products or services may be of benefit to you, give me just a few quick moments to share with you how we can help.
3.) Based on all that information, I'll be able to give you our best price in the whole world right down to the penny, the *first* time around.

Does that sound fair enough? (Wait and listen carefully)

Note

You must address the underlying question behind the objection and the emotional concerns which drive it. If you don't do this with every objection presented you risk:

- ‣ losing rapport
- ‣ missing opportunities to learn more about your client's real needs
- ‣ causing confusion or creating misunderstandings
- ‣ recognizing chances to up-sell
- ‣ not closing the sale
- ‣ not getting referrals
- ‣ increasing product or service returns
- ‣ heightened customer complaints

Be ready to handle every major objection a client has prior to their asking with scripted answers that are intelligible and fluid.

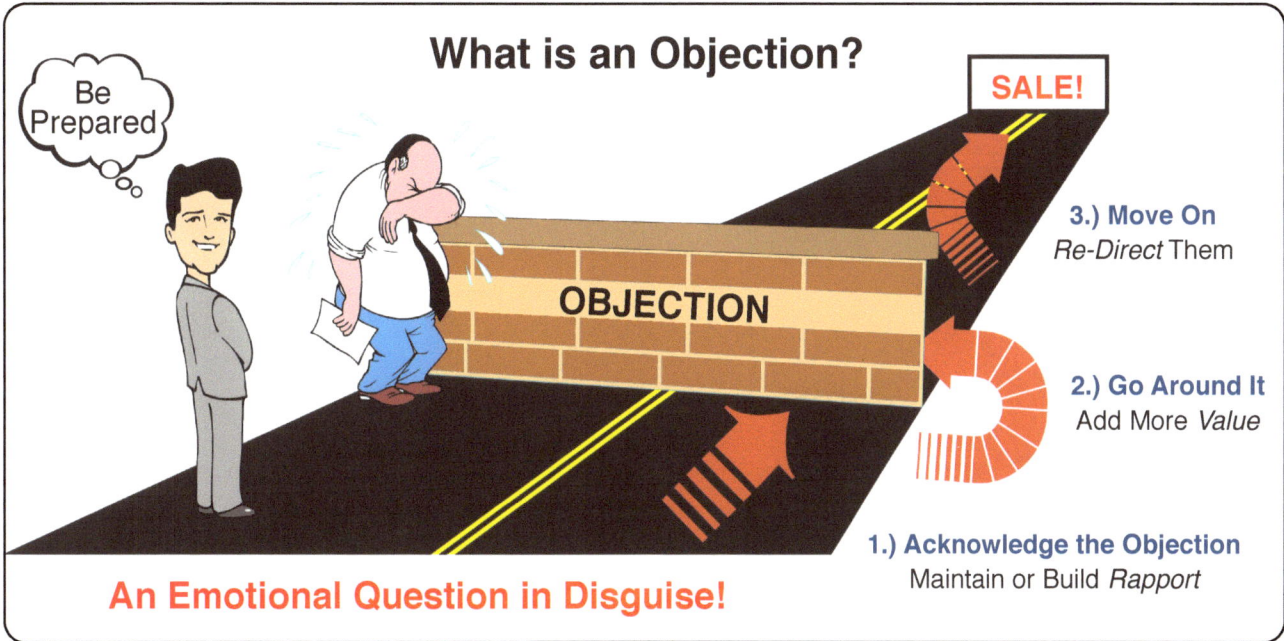

What is an Objection?

Be Prepared

SALE!

OBJECTION

3.) Move On
Re-Direct Them

2.) Go Around It
Add More *Value*

1.) Acknowledge the Objection
Maintain or Build *Rapport*

An Emotional Question in Disguise!

Objection
(An Emotional Question In Disguise)

_____
_____
_____
_____

1.) Acknowledge the Objection (Maintain or Build *Rapport*)

_____
_____
_____
_____

2.) Go Around It (Add More *Value*)

_____
_____
_____
_____

3.) Move On (*Re-Direct* Them)

_____
_____
_____
_____

The 'Precision Model' takes general objections (left hand) and focuses the client to provide specific answers (right hand). Place your hands together in front of you with your fingertips touching in a 'power position' and imagine holding the below conversation with a client.

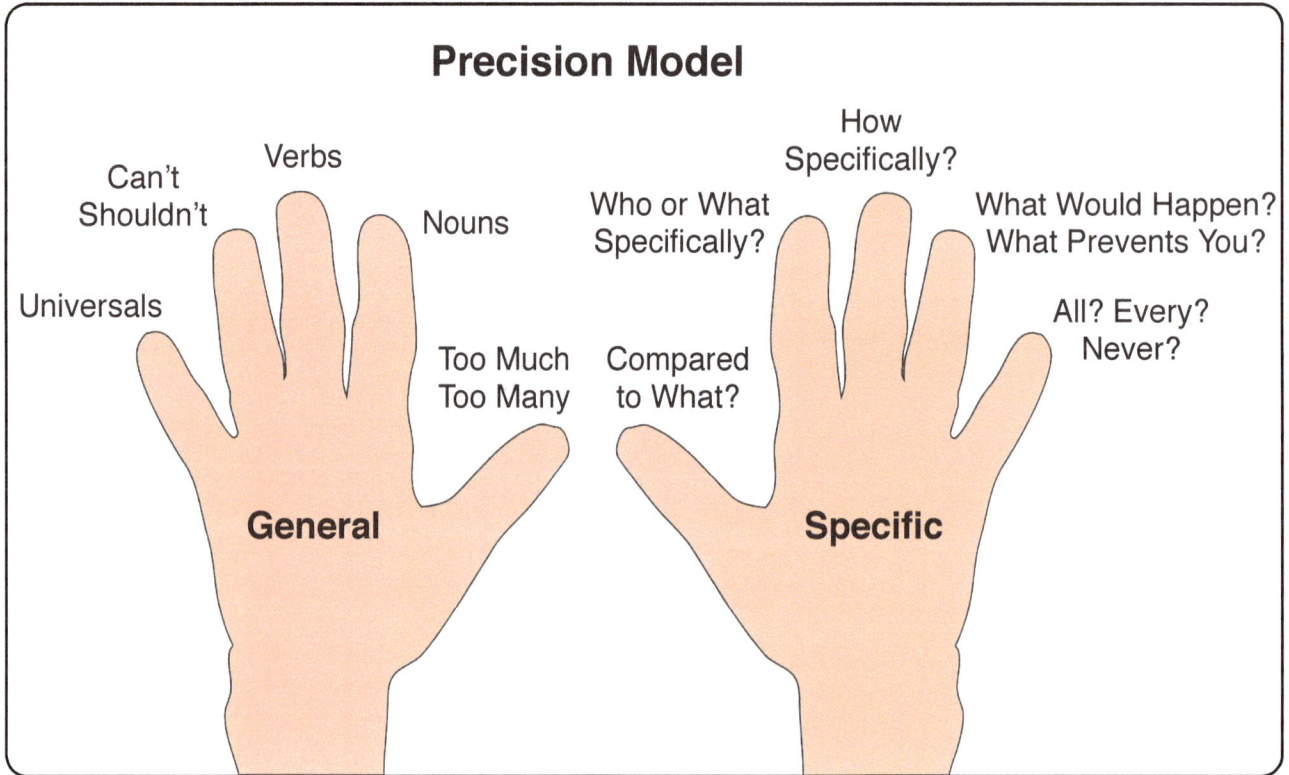

Precision Model

How Specifically?

Verbs

Can't Shouldn't

Nouns

Who or What Specifically?

What Would Happen? What Prevents You?

Universals

All? Every? Never?

Too Much Too Many

Compared to What?

General

Specific

Client	"Wow, your products or services just cost **too much**!"
You	"Really, may I ask, **in comparison to what**?"
Client	"In comparison to **someone's** advertisement I saw recently."
You	"Oh? **Who specifically** was running the ads to which you're referring?"
Client	"One of your competitors said we could **get these** products or services at a discount."
You	"**How specifically** would they have been able to accomplish that at these prices?"
Client	"Well, I guess I would have had to purchase a larger quantity to make that happen."
You	"I see. Wouldn't you prefer not having to spend additional money unnecessarily?"
Client	"Yes, I suppose so."
You	"Ok, well let's help you get your order started. Try our 'xyz' products or services for the next 30 days. I believe you'll find our customer support to be fantastic too."
Client	"I don't know . . . **I just can't**."
You	"**What would prevent you** from purchasing the products or services you need?"
Client	"I can **never** seem to find the sizes I'm looking for!"
You	"You can **never** find the sizes you're looking for?"
Client	"I couldn't find the 'size 50' products or services I needed during my last purchase."
You	"Great! We have the size 50 products or services in stock. Cash, check or credit?"

Who Do *They* Know?

Referrals

The most over-looked aspect in sales is asking for referrals. Regardless of whether you consummate a deal, ask everyone for at least 3 referrals. Begin asking yourself, for each of the people below, who do *they* know?

What about the People with whom I ...

Work?	Volunteer?	Am Related?
Go to Church?	Went to School?	Dance?
Exercise?	Used to Date?	Know Next Door?
Grew-up?	Use to Socialize?	Car Pool?

How about when I go to my ...

Dry cleaner?	Health Food Store?	Post Office?
Veterinarian?	Toy Store?	Masseuse?
Doctor?	Hotel?	Department Stores?
Dentist?	Bank or Credit Union?	Overnight Shipping?
Lawyer?	Telephone Company?	Health Organization?
Accountant?	Bakery?	Computer Store?
Library?	Deli?	Psychologist?
Insurance Office?	Furniture Store?	Plumber?
Grocery Store?	Appliance Store?	Bicycle Repair Shop?
Book Store?	Clothing Store?	Home Builder?
Florist?	Chiropractic Office?	Travel Agent?
Coffee Shop?	Beauty Salon?	Photography Studio?
Favorite Restaurant?	Tanning Office?	Temporary Agency?
Car & Truck Dealer?	Shoe Repair?	Landscape Company?
Mechanic?	Mortgage Company?	Graphics Designer?
Ski Resort?	Art Store?	Real Estate Developer?
Gym or Health Spa?	Nail Salon?	Heat / Air Conditioning?
Printer or Copier?	Auto Body Shop?	Real Estate Office?
Stock Broker?	Pawn Shop?	Title Insurance Company?
Pet Store?	Pharmacy?	Country Clerk Office?
Laundry Mat?	Locksmith?	Scuba Diving Store?

Who are People I know that ...

Use an iPhone?	On a Bowling Team?	Go Golfing?
Have an E-Mail?	Play an Instrument?	Play Soccer?
Own a Business?	Own a Home?	
Work with Animals?	Take Vitamins?	
Love to Ski?	Are in Sales?	Have Children?
Enjoy Traveling?	Like Chess?	Ride Bikes?

One-Minute Commercial

Get Ready!   **Get Permission!!**   **GO!!!**   **You __DID__ it!**

The "A-B-C" of selling is to "Always Be Closing". Therefore whenever someone asks you the infamous question 'so what do you do for a living?', you need to be prepared with a creative answer often referred to as an 'elevator pitch' or one-minute commercial.

Question "So, what do you do for a living?"

Answer "Oh, I show business owners how to get 10 years of advertising for the price of less than 1 year's worth of advertising."

Question (A little confused . . .) Really? How does that work?"

Answer "Well, it would take me *one-full minute* to explain my business to you. When would be the best time for us to get together when you'd be free for *one-full minute*?"

Question "Right now I guess. What is this? What are you talking about?"

Answer "Think about any major form of advertising, like newspaper, radio, yellow pages, TV, internet, fliers, coupons, billboards, etc. In all of those mediums you're paying for a space in time, whether it be for a day, a week or even a month. But when that fleeting moment passes - that's it! *(Snap fingers)* You're finished. You have to reach into your wallet and pay again, and again, and again. You see, I work for the world's largest sign company and we help business owners brand their company logo and get a beautiful outdoor lighted-electric sign and digital message-center with an unconditional guarantee against breakage for 10 years. Our clients only pay for this form of advertising once and it's out in front of their location working for them for over a decade - guaranteed. Their signs won't call in sick, they don't take vacations, and they work 24 hours a day, 365 days a year. It's the hardest working advertising employee they have! How many employees do you have like that?"

Warm Market

Working your warm market involves contacting and speaking to anyone with whom you have a modest relationship, including occasional friends, business associates and acquaintances.

Incorrect	Correct
Try to sell them over the phone.	1.) Engage in some brief, friendly small-talk
Talk on and on and on . . .	2.) Transfer your enthusiasm and ask for help
Avoid direct questions	3.) Compliment and encourage your client
Over-power your client	4.) Offer a disclaimer and an 'out'
Lose control of the conversation	5.) Close your objective; set an appointment

You "Hi [Client], it's [Your Name], how are you?"

Client "Oh hi, I'm fine thanks. What's going on?" **(1)** Engage in some relaxed small-talk.

You "[Client], **(2)** I was wondering if you could help me?" *(How?)* "**I need your opinion.** I'm really excited because I just started working for '123' company and they've asked me to give some in-home presentations as part of my training. **(3)** I know you're more of an expert when it comes things like this, and so I was hoping you would give me some feedback or pointers as to how I could improve my presentation. **(4)** Our products and services are not for everybody and you're certainly not under any obligation to purchase, but I was hoping you'd take a look?"

Client "Sure, why not. What is it?"

You "Ok, great! Well, that's what I want to *show* you, you certainly can't see it over the phone! **(5)** Would you like for me to stop by tonight or tomorrow morning?"

Advertising Market

Working your advertising market involves contacting and speaking to anyone who has responded to your various forms of advertisement such as newspaper ads or e-mail blasts.

You   "Hi, is [Client] available please?"

Client "Yes, this is [Client]."

You   "Hi [Client], my name is [Your Name] with '123' company. I saw you responded to our advertisement recently. Which of our products or services caught your attention?"

Client "Your new widget."

You   "Great! Well, we're very pleased that you contacted us and we're happy to be of help. How specifically were you planning on using our new widget?"

Client "I was planning on putting it in our guest bedroom."

You   "Ah, that's a perfect place for our new widget! Our 'x' model has shown to be very effective handling 'abc' situations with our clients." *(Give at least 3 testimonials)*

Client "Oh wow, that's pretty cool."

You   "[Client], we are running a promotional right now and, if you wish to take advantage of our special, we'd like to give you a free shiny gadget along with your new widget."

Client "A free shiny gadget in addition to my new widget? Ok!"

You   "Ok, fantastic! Since you'd enjoy receiving our widgets and gadgets immediately, to which mailing address would you like your products or services sent?"

Client "123 Anywhere Street . . ."

You   "Wonderful. And how would you like to process your order with us today? Cash, check or credit card please?"

Client "Credit Card."

You   "Thank you for your order, we value your business. [Client], may I ask, who do you know that might want to take advantage of this offer? If you can provide us with three friends who might like to try our widgets, we could help absorb your shipping costs!"

Cold Market

Working your cold market involves contacting and speaking to anyone who has neither contacted you or your company with an interest in your products or services nor was expecting to be contacted. A 'cold call' is when you make an unannounced introduction.

You "Hi, this is [Your Name] with '123' company. I was wondering, does your company offer 'xyz' products or services?"

Client "Yes, why do you ask?"

You "Well, this is a pretty tight market and an even tougher economy. We happen to build high-quality patented parts for the 'xyz' products or services you sell."

Client Really?

You "Yes, in fact I was hoping you would be kind enough to introduce me to the person in your organization who is responsible for making decisions with regards to the purchasing of parts for your 'xyz' products or services."

Client Please hold-- (The call is transferred)

You "Hi [Client], my name is [Your Name] with '123' company and we build parts for several of the 'xyz' products or services your company offers."

Owner "Thanks, but I just don't have a need for your parts at this time."

You "I understand. There's never a convenient time to look into manufacturing costs, especially during your busy season. But, please bear in mind, we can reduce your hard costs by as much as 30% which is not easily done in this competitive market."

Owner "Wait a minute, how can your parts save us 30% on our hard costs?"

You "Our patented designs remove the need for several expensive and out-dated components you currently use during your manufacturing process."

Owner "Can you stop by next Tuesday morning at 10am, I want to see your patents."

You "You bet. Will your business partners be joining us?"

Owner "No, I'm the sole owner - the buck stops with me."

You "Great, I'm looking forward to meeting you at your offices next Tuesday at 10 am."

Never Assume the Obvious

My mom's friend once tried to make a strawberry pie. Pleased with her creation, she asked me how it tasted. I said it was really good but, in all honestly, it could stand to be a little better if it had any strawberries in it. Confused and perplexed she looked at the recipe again and, although the title said 'strawberry pie', there were no strawberries listed in the ingredients. In addition to a great laugh we enjoy to this day, it taught me 'never assume the obvious'.

Outside-Sales Prospecting

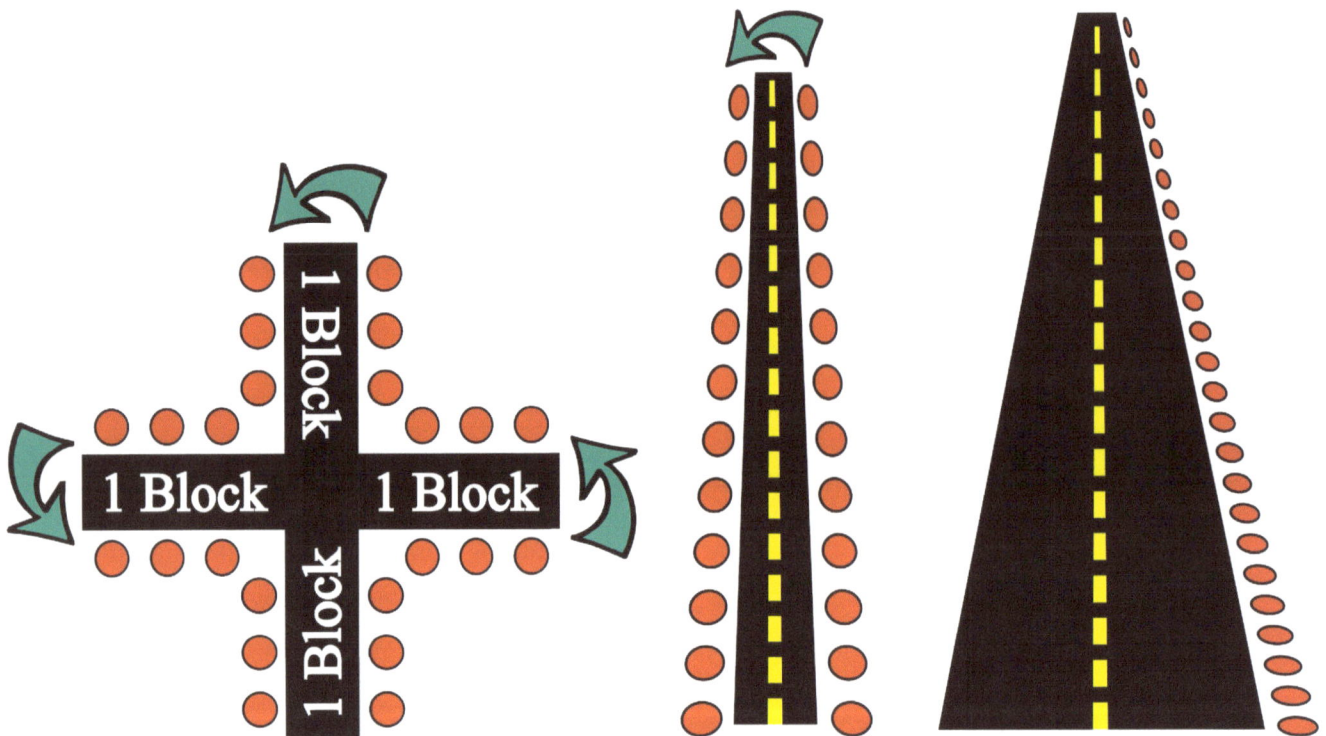

Intersections

If you are working in a downtown area or smaller rural community, you may find the need to 'work your intersections'. Park your car, open that two-thousand pound car door and make a list of the first three businesses in all directions from the center of an intersection. Doing so will quickly provide you with a list of 24 prospects with whom you can introduce yourself.

Straight-Aways

If you are working a long boulevard or secondary highway, you may find the need to 'work the roads'. As you are driving, carefully make a list of 12 businesses on one-side of the street. Then, depending on the type of road, flip a u-turn and finish your list in the other direction.

Work to the Opportunity

We all have a propensity to stay in our comfort zones in much the same fashion as **heaters** and **air-conditioners** help to keep our homes agreeable. If your sales performance is slacking and you're out of your comfort zone falling behind on your bills, have you ever noticed that your proverbial sales **heater** miraculously kicks in? Suddenly you're focused, attentive and deliver convincing presentations which produce sales!

Once you've reached your sales goals you feel great, your boss is off your back and you're ahead of your bills. Returning to work to 'grind out' your day becomes entirely distasteful and your proverbial sales **air-conditioner** kicks in. Suddenly you feel compelled to celebrate by catching a quick round of golf or a few drinks at that newly opened bar with your friends.

If you are to achieve your goals and dreams in life, using sales as your vehicle, then you have to work to the opportunity provided by your company and the market place. Be careful not to stray into the Pavlovian sell - spend response. Remember, it's not how much you earn that matters, it's your ability to save, re-invest or plant for future growth that counts. How do you do this exactly? Ask yourself if you want to be 'golfing for life' at age 45 or a caddy at age 60.

"Cherry Picking"

'Cherry picking' is a sales term used to describe outside-sales people who call on businesses which they believe have the greatest chance of purchasing their products or services. Hence they drive by and 'pick the cherry' which appears to be the most ripe and delicious on the tree. Don't leave the rest of the fruit for the laborers who will patiently work the orchard after you!

Suits

"If you sold suits, to whom would you sell them? To a man or woman who owned no suits or to someone who had a closet full of suits? Who would have the greater appreciation for suits, the person who does not own one or the person who has a closet full and enjoys talking about, looking at, buying and wearing new suits?" *People who wear suits, buy suits!*

Stay in Your Day

"All you can do is all you can do, and that is good enough." Imagine holding a solid-silver tray with both hands. Feel the weight of responsibility in your arms as the stack grows high with bills, debts and financial obligations you owe. Set that tray down and put your worries off to the side! In your mind's eye demand those bills be there when you return to collect them this evening. Be vigilant to dole your time and energy on only those activities which statistically will alleviate the challenges from which you are currently worried. Stay in your day!

Name _____   **Month** _____ **, 20**_____

	Monday	Tuesday	Wednesday	Thursday	Friday	Saturday	Weekly Total
Introductions	/	/	/	/	/	/	/
Presentations	/	/	/	/	/	/	/
Closes	/	/	/	/	/	/	/
Sales	/	/	/	/	/	/	/
Volume	$	$	$	$	$	$	$
Commission	$	$	$	$	$	$	$

	Monday	Tuesday	Wednesday	Thursday	Friday	Saturday	Weekly Total
Introductions	/	/	/	/	/	/	/
Presentations	/	/	/	/	/	/	/
Closes	/	/	/	/	/	/	/
Sales	/	/	/	/	/	/	/
Volume	$	$	$	$	$	$	$
Commission	$	$	$	$	$	$	$

	Monday	Tuesday	Wednesday	Thursday	Friday	Saturday	Weekly Total
Introductions	/	/	/	/	/	/	/
Presentations	/	/	/	/	/	/	/
Closes	/	/	/	/	/	/	/
Sales	/	/	/	/	/	/	/
Volume	$	$	$	$	$	$	$
Commission	$	$	$	$	$	$	$

	Monday	Tuesday	Wednesday	Thursday	Friday	Saturday	Weekly Total
Introductions	/	/	/	/	/	/	/
Presentations	/	/	/	/	/	/	/
Closes	/	/	/	/	/	/	/
Sales	/	/	/	/	/	/	/
Volume	$	$	$	$	$	$	$
Commission	$	$	$	$	$	$	$

	Monday	Tuesday	Wednesday	Thursday	Friday	Saturday	Weekly Total
Introductions	/	/	/	/	/	/	/
Presentations	/	/	/	/	/	/	/
Closes	/	/	/	/	/	/	/
Sales	/	/	/	/	/	/	/
Volume	$	$	$	$	$	$	$
Commission	$	$	$	$	$	$	$

	Monthly Total
Introductions	/
Presentations	/
Closes	/
Sales	/
Volume	$
Commission	$

Average Commission Earned Per	
Introduction	$
Presentation	$
Close	$
Sale	$

Plan Your Work and Work Your Plan

The monthly calendar provided, which I have used both for myself and my sales teams for over two decades, provides an excellent means of viewing daily, weekly and monthly performance on a single page. Excluding weekends and holidays, there are at least 20 working days in any calendar month. Plan your work for the month by writing down your individual goals including the number of introductions, presentations, closes and sales which you are committing to achieve. Work your plan to the best of your ability and track your performance (and that of your sales people) on a daily, weekly and month-end basis.

Lead by Example

"People don't do what you say, they do what you do." For those with children, you know this statement to be true! You have to lead by example. Managers often make the mistake of hanging up their sales hat when they sit down into that nice comfortable chair. Get up off your butt, role up your sleeves, put some elbow grease into your work and keep your hands dirty.

I have found the most beneficial aspect of this performance tracking calendar to be the section in the bottom right-hand corner entitled, "Average Commission Earned Per". When you *know* (and can consistently document) that you will earn "x" amount of dollars every time you give a qualified prospect a formal introduction, you develop tremendous peace-of-mind when going about your daily business routine. If you don't track your numbers and those of your sales people, you cannot adequately convey this type of confidence to yourself or them. Lead by example, use this calendar and experience its power.

Managing Your Sales People

"People don't do what you expect, they do what you inspect." I was known for holding the following conversation with my sales people. Older reps would often giggle when they heard me having this conversation with newer reps:

Manager *(After any small talk)* "So, what were your numbers today?"
Sales "Well, here's the deal..."
Manager "Nope. I don't need a deal, just the numbers."
Sales "But it's an interesting story. You see -- "
Manager *(Interrupting)* "--My little form here only allows me to enter a number, not a story."
Sales "Oh."
Manager "Your numbers will tell me the entire story. So, what were your numbers today?"

Please, never ask a sales person '*"what did you sell today"?* No matter who you are, not every day is a sales day and answering 'nothing' is devastating. Ask, *"how was your day"?*

Helpful Quotes

The following is a list of quotes which have most impacted my sales career:

"Be a professional. Not every dentist feels like waking up in the morning and putting their hands into someone else's dirty mouth to clean it. Rise above your temporary emotional state of mind and do what needs to be done in the moment." - Brian Kornuth

"Let your customer help change your mood by becoming involved in their business and helping improve their lives. Soon you'll find yourself forgetting about your own concerns and moving on with your day. Nothing feels better than to take a deep breath, put a big smile on your face, extend your hand and greet your next client with a warm welcome." - Tom Johnson

"People don't care how much you know, until they know how much you care. Make a friend before you make a sale." - Kozy Boren

"To become a master in any field, you have to master the basics. Perform the fundamentals of your business until it's second nature and then you're unstoppable." - Jim Callahan

"I always recalled the expression, 'the view never changes unless you're a leader'. So we're on the leading edge not the bleeding edge; we lead by innovation not imitation." - Tom Boren

"If you don't say it straight, it comes out crooked." - Vernie Boren

"If you want to sell larger orders, then you have to present them. It doesn't pay to go elephant hunting all day, but you'll never catch one looking for deer." - Buddy Swisshelm

"I was recently asked how I've been able to run over 100 marathons in my life. Well, first I had to stand up because it's difficult to run a marathon sitting down. Then I leaned forward until I started to fall and, not wanting to hit the ground, I placed one foot in front of the other. I just kept falling forward catching myself until I crossed the finish line." - Tom Johnson

"Don't loose your joy." - Rick Knight

"Thinking is the hardest work there is, which the probable reason why so few people engage in it." - Henry Ford

"The past doesn't equal the future." - Anthony Robbins

"When written in Chinese, the word 'crisis' is composed of two characters - one represents danger and the other represents opportunity." - John F Kennedy

Four Levels of Learning

1.) Unconscious Incompetence - When you were a little kid and your parents placed you in the back seat of their car and strapped you in with a seatbelt, you were unaware (unconscious) that you didn't know how to drive a car (incompetence). In fact, the thought of driving had never even crossed your mind as it was something only your parents or grown-ups did.

2.) Conscious Incompetence - However one day, perhaps as you reached the age of a young teenager, the thought suddenly entered your mind, "Maybe one day I could be driving a car too!" And in that moment you become aware (conscious) of the fact that you didn't know how to drive a car (incompetence). Whereas you had never considered driving before, now you had an awareness that maybe one-day you would.

3.) Conscious Competence - At the age of 15.5 you might have begun taking driving lessons using a temporary permit. Many states in the U.S. allow for a 15.5 year-old to begin driving so long as a licensed adult driver is present in the vehicle while they are practicing. Do you remember the first time you tried (conscious) to release the clutch and excel up a hill in a car (competence)? It took ever amount of energy and concentration you could muster to avoid stalling the engine.

4.) Unconscious Competence - But now that you have been driving for a number of years, you no longer have to think (unconscious) about driving a car (competence) anymore. You could be changing the channel on your radio while eating a hamburger and not give a second that to shifting gears at the same time.

You're currently in at least stage 2 of mastering the sales process, or you wouldn't be aware that you wanted to read this book. If you have been practicing some of the exercises contained in this book, then you are at least in stage 3. Stage 3 is where you must put in the necessary time and energy to become proficient in these skills. And when you reach the point where these sales skills become 'second nature' to you, you will have arrived at stage 4 and possess 'unconscious competence'. At that time you can focus solely on those activities which are most likely to bring the results you desire.

Follow Your Dreams

"If you build it they will come." Some people grasped the film 'Field of Dreams', others didn't. If you didn't see the film or didn't quite understand it, the point was simple and beautiful. Have the conviction and the courage to follow your dreams. Pursue that which you love and know to be true for what you are seeking will materialize in due season. *Mastering the Sales Process* can allow all your dreams to come true!

Plantronics
SAVI W720 Model Headsets

I would feel remise if I did not give mention to the best performing headsets on the market. Next to your (Apple) computer, the primary tool of the trade for any inside-sales person is your headset. There's just nothing worse than getting a severe migraine headache from the weight of a heavy or poorly adjustable headset. And if you've ever had to struggle hearing your clients (or have them hear your) against a noisy back-drop, it can be down-right infuriating.

My experience has shown Plantronics to build high-quality and dependable headset devices. I currently make use of the **Plantronics SAVI W720** model (left). I like this design for several key reasons. First, it features dual-ear listening capabilities. The adage, "you have two ears and one mouth so that you can listen twice as much as you talk" is as much applicable to sales as any other industry. The volume is very powerful and can compete with even the most nerve-racking environments. The unit boasts nine (9) hours of talk time and is true to its claim. The noise-canceling microphone differentiates your voice from ambient sounds and delivers clear audio to your clients. This particular model works seamlessly with a traditional (ground-line) telephone, a computer (ie. Skype), and a cell phone (with Blue Tooth technology) all with the simple touch of a button on the base. It has an impressive range of 100 meters (300 Feet) which has allowed me the opportunity to make many a pot of coffee without interrupting my work-flow. If this particular headset had a down-side, it might be that the audio function does not bode well for music. Meaning, it's not exactly made for you to jam-out to your music in iTunes. Given this is a professional headset built for telecommunications, the speaker ranges are designed for the human voice and not songs in your favorites list. The higher price may be a factor for some, but the product is excellent and worthy of mention, which should encourage you to at least investigate the Plantronics product line which can easily be found by running a search for dealers online:

http://www.plantronics.com/us/product/savi-700?skuId=sku5800021

Please note that this model can be found for sale online for around $250 per unit; so don't mind the Plantronic's sticker price of $422. For example, see this link:

http://www.amazon.com/Plantronics-Savi-W720-Multi-Device-Wireless/dp/B005FSJ6PM